British Library cataloguing-in-Publication Data
A catalogue record for this book is available from the British Library.

ACC Art Books Ltd
www.antiquecollectorsclub.com

Sandy Lane, Old Martlesham,
Woodbridge, Suffolk IP12 4SD, UK
Tel: 01394 389950 Fax: 01394 389999
Email: info@antique-acc.com
or
ACC Distribution,
6 West 18th Street, Suite 4B,
New York, NY 10011, USA
Tel: 212 645 1111 Fax: 212 989 3205
Email: sales@antiquecc.com

The cover pattern is reproduced from History, a Dent's Everyman series
wood engraving, 1935
Endpapers are reproduced from the Dunbar Hay 'Doll's House' trade card, 1938
Opposite and page 23, undated illustrated letter and Christmas card from Ravilious
Page 5, Wedgwood ceramics back stamp, 1930s

Published by ACC Art Books Ltd., Woodbridge, England
Design by Webb & Webb Design Limited, London
Printed and bound in Slovenia

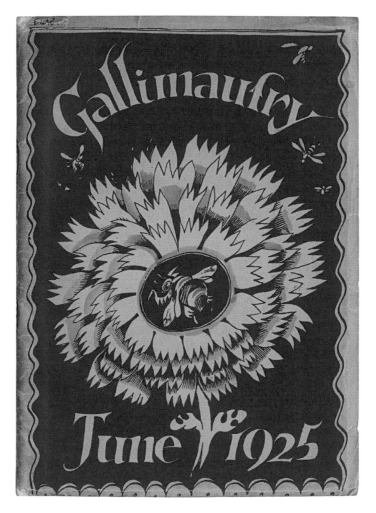

The Gallimaufry, A new magazine of the students of the RCA which will appear for this once only, June 1925. Edited by Douglas Percy Bliss, the cover illustration, a line drawing by Ravilious, has colour added by hand and contains illustrations by Edward Bawden (hand-coloured in their Redcliffe Road lodgings by Bliss, Ravilious and Bawden), and wood-engravings by Ravilious and Enid Marx.

E ric Ravilious was the son of a small town shopkeeper obsessed
by a puritanical Old Testament God. Although he managed
to break away from many of the trappings of his boyhood,
both the love of everyday household things, and an enduring
sense of sin – which he frequently contravened – remained constant
factors in his all-too-short life. The origins of the family are obscure;
the name Ravilious being thought to be of Huguenot origin. However,
by the end of the nineteenth century several members of the family
were living in Acton, then a still rural community on the Middlesex
side of London, where Eric's father, Frank, opened an upholstery
business, two of his uncles being tailors in the immediate vicinity.
Shortly after Eric's birth his father panicked, having over-ordered
some item of stock – mattresses has been suggested – and declared
himself bankrupt, thereafter he moved to Eastbourne where he
opened what was grandly described as an antique business, but
in the absence of funds this was probably initially more nearly
equivalent to the French *brocante*, trading in house clearance and
second-hand goods, many of which would today be regarded as
desirable antiques. Thus, young Eric grew up surrounded by an
intriguing, if motley, array of bric-a-brac of the sort that was to
inspire a number of artists and writers of his generation, and it is
not altogether surprising that among his earliest surviving drawings
are studies of a pair of boots and a teapot. In later life, such everyday
objects were to reappear not only in his watercolours but also in
designs for ceramics and textiles.

His clean, neat drawings attracted the attention of his teachers and at
the suggestion of the headmaster of the Municipal Secondary School
he transferred in 1919 to Eastbourne School of Art, from which
he won a £60 two year scholarship to the Royal College of Art in
London. He enrolled in September 1922 and was assigned to the

Design School, the same day as Edward Bawden, and an instant friendship was struck. Although totally different in character – Ravilious was gregarious, sporting and fun-loving, while Bawden was introverted and unsociable – they came from similar nonconformist shop-keeping backgrounds. Their work and lives were to be inextricably intertwined for the next twenty years. Of equal importance, at least in the short-term, was the friendship of another new entrant, Douglas Percy Bliss, a more mature student who had already gained a degree in English Literature before enrolling in the Painting School at the RCA. Bliss not only guided the younger men's reading, he began to research the history of wood-engraving, an art-form in which Ravilious was to excel, and edited the student magazine *Gallimaufry* in 1925, which had a decorative pen-drawn device by Ravilious on the cover and included an impression of one of his early engravings, *Sussex Church*.

As the initial grant from Eastbourne was for two years only, rather than the full three-year course, Ravilious had to complete his Diploma in this time, and chose mural decoration as his special subject. In the interest of speed, he eschewed the laborious historic techniques as practised by Cennino Cennini and taught by Professor Tristram, opting instead for a mixture of gesso powder and ordinary colour, producing what Bawden later described as 'a big gay painting that really had some pretensions to being a mural.'[1] His success won him the Design School Travelling Scholarship with the result that he spent the summer of 1924 in Florence, and on his return extra funds were made available, enabling him to remain at the College for a further year and complete the course. This extra year was to have a lasting effect on his work as the Principal, William Rothenstein, had persuaded Paul Nash to join the College staff on a part-time basis and teach in the Design School. Nash had recently taken up wood-engraving and had also started to design pattern papers for the Curwen Press, a practice that he said enabled him to explore abstract pattern without compromising his more figurative work; a discipline he later extended to include the designing of textiles.

In the 1920s those students who were awarded Travelling Scholarships were expected to use their time in Italy making copies of early Italian paintings, but Ravilious seems to have totally disregarded this requirement; the only surviving pictorial records from this

Sussex Church, an early Ravilious engraving of Lullington Church near Eastbourne, printed in *Gallimaufry*, 1925; Ravilious had returned from Italy with three completed engravings the previous year. This illustration is described in the magazine as a woodcut – a general description of wood-engravings (cut on the endgrain) and woodcuts (cut on the plank) in the 1920s.

sojourn being three wood-engravings, *Road at Florence, San Gimignano* and *Woodland Outside Florence*, his most ambitious engravings to date. However, it became clear in 1928 when he, Edward Bawden and Charles Mahoney were commissioned to paint murals for Morley College that he had not wasted his time.

The Morley commission arose in the wake of the unveiling of Rex Whistler's mural, *In Pursuit of Rare Meats*, in the Tate Gallery's Restaurant, which had been paid for by the art dealer Sir Joseph Duveen. Whistler having been a pupil of Professor Tonks' at the Slade, Rothenstein immediately approached Duveen to see if he would fund a similar project to be carried out by Royal College students. Duveen agreed and Charles Aitken, the Director of the Tate – or The National Gallery of British Art as it was then known – suggested Morley College for Working Men and Women in South London as an institution worthy of being the recipient for such a project. Morley College had been founded by Lilian Baylis in the late 1880s, and for the first decades of its existence had shared premises with the Old Vic Theatre, only moving in 1924 to premises of its own – a converted Georgian property in nearby Westminster Bridge Road. Once agreement for the murals was reached, Ravilious and Bawden were assigned the three walls of the Refreshment Room, the other wall being mainly windows, in a newly built extension to the rear of the main building. Mahoney was given the task of decorating the wall behind the stage in the Assembly Hall. The theme originally suggested to Ravilious and Bawden was 'London', but this was quickly abandoned in favour of 'fantasy', which, for the two main walls – they were allotted one each – developed into an exploration of sixteenth-century literature and drama. This was a tribute both to Douglas Percy Bliss, whose knowledge of English literature had guided much of their reading and enthusiasms, and to the pioneering work of Lilian Baylis and the Old Vic in the Shakespearean revival.

Writing nearly half-a-century later Bawden credited Ravilious with devising the overall plan: 'Whatever beneficial influence Italy had had on Eric was now to some extent revealed, not by plagiarism,

Detail of a watercolour design for the Morley College murals, 1928. The tiered pavilion illustrates Ben Jonson's play, *The Sad Shepherd*, with the Long Man of Wilmington and Sussex Downs in the background.

rather by his skill in organising space and creating figures to be
sent dancing and swinging in ballet movements across the walls.'[2]
Dividing the wall surface into separate compartments was typical of
Italian frescoes of the thirteenth and fourteenth centuries, a pictorial
device that enabled the artists to depict the life of Christ, the
apostles and saints, through a sequence of pertinent incidents and
miracles. And as by this date the churches were almost invariably
high structures, it was often necessary for the frescoists to work in
layers depicting one scene above another. Exploiting his memory
of Florentine frescoes, Ravilious devised a unifying framework of
scaffold, open staging and pavilions to supply the overall structure
for the two long walls, but in their final realisation his design owed
as much to the then still extant cast-iron piers at Eastbourne, Brighton
and Hastings as to Gaddi and Giotto. The format, however, was
successful, enabling the two men to unite diverse subjects into
a coherent whole. On the long east wall Ravilious created three
pavilions: the one on the left containing scenes from Christopher
Marlowe's *Dr Faustus*; the centre one, scenes from *The Arraignment of Paris*
by George Peele and *Cynthia's Revels* by Jonson; and the right-hand
one, Jonson's *Sad Shepherd*. Interspersed with these was a seemingly
random selection of vines, a palm tree and an Elizabethan masque,
as well as a large naked figure of Venus, plus Pomona, goddess of
fruitful abundance, and the Long Man of Wilmington. For his second
wall, he adapted the open-stage format in order to depict the interior
of a London lodging house. In contrast to the 'dancing and swinging'
figures that sprang across the long wall, he here exploited a narrower
vertical space, showing the interior of the lodging house as though
it were an open doll's house, each room complete with its furniture
and occupants, while in the centre his future wife, Tirzah Garwood —
the inspiration for both Venus and Pomona — climbs the staircase
connecting the different levels. 'Elizabethan plays, Shakespeare,
Olympian gods and goddesses, Punch and Judy, a Miracle play
and a doll's house — Gosh! what a riot it was'[3] was how Bawden
summed up their joint Morley experience years later.

The work was spread out over a couple of years and the murals
were finally unveiled on 6th February 1930 by the former — and
future — Prime Minister, Stanley Baldwin, whose Parliamentary
Private Secretary, Sir Geoffrey Fry, made the necessary arrangements.
Fry and his wife became friends of the Raviliouses, inviting them

Tennis was one of Ravilious's favourite sports, his scrapbooks contain
many newspaper cuttings of tennis players. As a result of his work on the
Morley College mural, Sir Geoffrey Fry, Stanley Baldwin's private secretary,
commissioned a series of tempera painted door panels for the living room of
his Portman Square, London flat in 1930. The designs were first illustrated in
Colour Schemes for the Modern Home, 1933.

In 1929, at the time he was painting *Dr Faustus Conjuring Mephistopheles* in a section of the Morley College mural, Ravilious cut an engraving of Faustus for *The Legion Book*, published for the Prince of Wales to raise money for The British Legion. The book included contributions from more than 30 authors and 17 artists, including Edward Bawden, and was printed at the Curwen Press.

for weekends at their Wiltshire home and commissioning Eric in 1932 to paint three decorative door panels, depicting a mixed doubles at tennis, for their London flat. The following year Ravilious received two further mural commissions, but like those at Morley they were destined to be short-lived. Morley College was bombed during the Blitz in 1940 and completely destroyed, while the mural for the Tea Room – a circular structure – in Oliver Hill's newly built Midland Hotel, Morecambe, deteriorated beyond repair due to residual damp in the walls. The subject of this mural was a seaside promenade with elegant trelliswork, arches and pavilions, seen against a skyline reflecting the twenty-four hour cycle of morning, noon and night. Night provided him with the excuse to introduce a glorious firework display of Venetian proportions – one of his favourite decorative motifs – combining the excuse for flourish, pattern and sparkle, elements that recur frequently in his wood-engravings. His only other mural, which depicted an underwater scene of ruined arches and seaweeds, was in the Victoria Pier Pavilion at Colwyn Bay, on the Welsh coast, which was painted over during the war. Recently careful removal of layers of overpaint has revealed a small section of this mural, but whether it is recoverable to any degree remains a moot point. Tirzah helped him with both these murals, which, unlike those at Morley, were designed to give maximum visual pleasure with a minimum of detailed figurative work, thus drastically cutting the time needed to paint them.

Ravilious adapted the open stage device, which he had exploited so successfully at Morley – and which appealed to the story-teller in him – for his 1929 wood-engraving *Faustus Conjuring Mephistopheles*. Pomona who, with her attendants, floated through the air above the Refreshment Room door, became a prototype for a number of other airborne figures at that time such as *Muse*, a bookmark for the Westminster Bank, commissioned through the Curwen Press in 1928, and his illustration to Harold Monro's poem, *Elm Angel*, number 26 in Faber & Faber's *Ariel Poems* series, also printed at Curwen. Such floating figures, both animal and human, also form essential elements in his engravings for the 1929 Lanston Monotype Corporation *Almanack*, enabling him to incorporate the signs of the Zodiac into appropriate Sussex settings: thus Aquarius pours water over one of the Downland churches, Taurus charges towards the

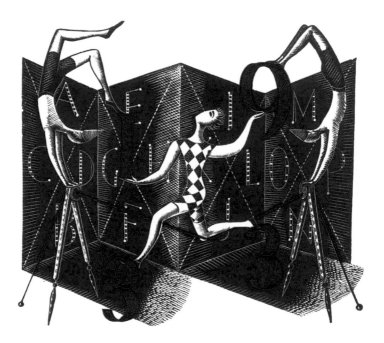

January. Beatrice Warde, the Monotype Corporation's publicity manager, commissioned Ravilious to engrave an illustrated A to Z as a set of calendar type specimen cards, with each card set in a different Monotype typeface (January set in Gill Sans, Mono series 231) for 1933. The sporting and gymnastic figures closely resemble his sprites, cut for *Twelfth Night*. The figures illustrating December (see page 43) wear pagan-like holly and mistletoe head-dresses, a theme Ravilious echoed in his large *November 5th, 1933*, painting.

Long Man of Wilmington, and Pegasus flies over the chalkpit above Bopeep near the East Sussex village of Alciston. The most endearing figure in the *Almanack* is that of Andromeda, whom he chose in preference to the traditional crab to represent Cancer: recently released by Perseus this lightly clad young lady – the broken chains still dangling from her ankles – balances precariously on a ladder as she ineffectually adjusts the tarpaulin on a freshly made hayrick.

The 1933 Monotype Calendar, created for the same firm, is Ravilious's most joyfully eccentric production. It was issued as twelve separate postcards printed with a second colour in addition to black, each card depicting puppet-like figures frolicking among lower case letter forms – the Monotype Corporation being the principal supplier of type-setting equipment for books and general printing purposes. The most ingenious of these figures is that for June – a solo performer juggling six hoops representing the letter 'O'.

Much of Ravilious's design-work was grounded in his skill as an engraver, but as Robert Harling noted perceptively: 'he was always, and above all, a designer who was also an engraver'.[4] He was interested in pattern and the textural effects that could be achieved by employing such simple means as a woodblock and graver. Like Thomas Bewick, the greatest wood engraver this country has ever produced, he was a white line engraver delighting in the contrast between line and ground, which he exploited to give an illusion of richness and colour. However, he also revelled in the creation of pattern for pattern's sake, and in this he was influenced by the fifteenth-century metal cuts, or dotted prints, to which Bliss had introduced him, and which he studied in the Print Room at the British Museum. In addition to the fact that Bliss was already researching his *A History of Wood Engraving* (published by Dent in 1928), Ravilious was encouraged to make use of the facilities of the Print Room by Laurence Binyon, the Keeper, whose daughter, Helen, was a fellow student. Study of these early German prints in the *manière criblée* encouraged his experimentation with dappling – the creation of a multitude of white dots, stars and florets – which he would exploit as a contrast to areas of rich blackness, as in his cover designs for the BBC's talks pamphlet, *British Art* and *The Curwen Press News Letter*, No.6.

Just as at Morecambe he had created swirling patterns out of the
giant firework display, exploiting the trajectory of rockets and the
rotating discs of Catherine Wheels, to give an air of light-hearted
exuberance, so in his vignettes he exploited pattern to achieve a
similar sense of joy, but in miniature. These vignettes have their
roots in old-fashioned printers' flowers, created to distract the eye
and embellish unsightly areas on the blank page. They first appear
in Martin Armstrong's *Desert, a Legend* published by Jonathan Cape in
1926, at the time when Paul Nash's influence on his work was at its
strongest. He developed one of these vignettes, *The Indestructible Beauty
of a Diamond*, into the motif of his Curwen Press pattern paper, his
earliest exercise in lithography, while others were to decorate the
dust-jackets of the Everyman's Library editions of the classics,
published by J.M. Dent. Small as many of these devices are they
always transmit a sense of energy and movement, being based
mostly on natural forms, leaves, shells, stars and ribbons, interfolding
and self-contained. They are indicative of the sheer joy he derived
from the physical act of engraving, but his masterpieces in this
medium are undoubtedly the illustrations to the Golden Cockerel
Press's limited edition *Twelfth Night or What You Will* (1932) and the
two volumes of *The Writings of Gilbert White of Selborne*, published by
the Nonesuch Press in 1938. These were always expensive books,
published in limited numbers and aimed at the connoisseur collector.

In contrast to such bibliophile editions, *High Street*, illustrated
through the medium of colour lithography, was published in 1938
by *Country Life* in a popular edition of two thousand copies, retailing
at seven shillings and sixpence (37.5p in today's money). Apart from
his 1927 Curwen Pattern Paper, Ravilious at this time had little
first-hand experience of lithography, except for the large print,
Newhaven Harbour, he had made the previous year for Contemporary
Lithographs, a company set up by Robert Wellington and John Piper.
Newhaven Harbour, which he described as a homage to Seurat was drawn
directly onto the stone, but with twenty-four plates for *High Street* this
was not practicable, so he had to draw these on metal lithographic
plates, a process he was to repeat early in the war with his series
of submarine prints. *High Street* was printed at the Curwen Press, but

*Curwen Pattern Paper, 1927, used for the cover of Eric Ravilious 1903–1942
Arts Council Memorial Exhibition, 1949.*

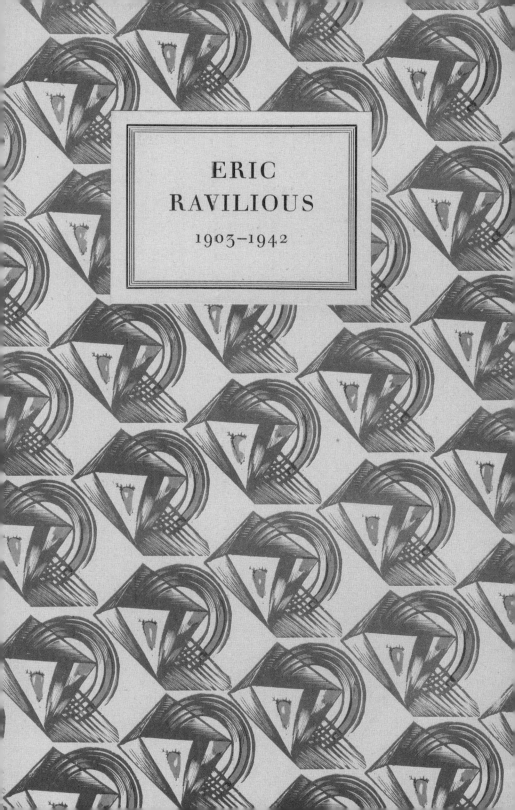

ERIC
RAVILIOUS

1903–1942

Garden tableware. Original design in pencil and watercolour and 13-inch transfer printed oval serving plate, 1939. Ravilious wrote to Helen Binyon that Wedgwood thought his designs 'above the heads of their customers and that safer designs should be tried first.'

for the submarine prints he worked directly, and experimentally, at Cowell's of Ipswich, controlling the proofing machines himself, which enabled him to vary the tints. If he had lived he would almost certainly have used the same technique for the projected Puffin Picture Book devoted to the chalk figures of the South Downs, which he was planning in collaboration with Noel Carrington.

Transfer printing was an essential part of the process for decorating china so, with his newly perfected skills as a lithographer, it is not surprising that his talents attracted the attention of both Tom Wedgwood and his cousin Josiah Wedgwood V, the Managing Director of the family firm. Both Noel Carrington and Cecilia Dunbar Kilburn, a friend from Royal College days, claimed to have introduced Ravilious to the Wedgwoods and on his first visit to Etruria he clearly got on well with Josiah, whom he described as being a fusion of 'the business man and the man of taste'.[5] The immediate result of this visit was a commission to design a mug for the impending coronation of King Edward VIII. Typically, Ravilious incorporated fireworks into his design along with the lion and unicorn, the royal initials 'ER' – for Edwardius Rex – and the date, 1937. It is recorded that Mrs Simpson was among the first customers to purchase one of these mugs from Dunbar Hay, the Mayfair shop founded by Cecilia Dunbar Kilburn and Athole Hay, the Registrar of the Royal College of Art. Following Edward VIII's abdication in favour of his brother, the mug was reissued with a 'G' for George replacing Edward's 'E'. The mug was reissued again in 1953, this time with the 'E' reinstated, for the coronation of Queen Elizabeth II. Throughout the English-speaking world, Ravilious's Coronation mug remains one of the best known ceramic designs of the twentieth century.

Following this success other designs for Wedgwood followed, though he was only ever responsible for the decoration and not for the ceramic forms, which were largely dictated by Keith Murray and Victor Skellern, thus his *Boat Race Day* design appears both on the rather cumbersome egg-cup-shaped vase as well as on the more elegant punch bowl. Among his best known designs are those for the *Alphabet* mug, exploiting both his characteristic capital letters and appropriate symbols, and the three dinner services – *Garden,* with its elegant array of tools, wheelbarrows and other related subjects, *Travel*, with vignettes of trains, aeroplanes, yachts and balloons, and the less specific *Persephone*. He also designed *Afternoon Tea*, a refined service of cups, saucers, small plates, sugar bowl, etc. *Travel*, which was manufactured in a rather unappealing grey, was not put into general production until 1953, eleven years after Ravilious's death.

Like his friend Edward Bawden, Ravilious was always happy to recycle a good image: two of the Travel vignettes had appeared earlier, the aeroplane as an illustration to Martin Armstrong's *Fifty-four Conceits* and the snowstorm – presumably intended to bring travel to a halt – in the *Kynoch Press Note Book*, both of 1933. The train scenes too were adapted from one of his engraved illustrations to L.A.G. Strong's *The Hansom Cab and the Pigeons*. The transfer process, through which these designs were were adapted, involved one of Wedgwood's craftsmen re-engraving them onto copper plates; impressions were then taken on special paper and the paper applied to each object – plate, mug or jug – after its initial biscuit firing, but before the addition of the glaze and colouring. The second firing would burn away the paper, leaving the finished article ready for the market.

It was Ravilious's skill as a lithographer, as much as his talent for design, that recommended him to the Wedgwoods, indeed, in a letter to Helen Binyon he reported that the family thought his designs above the heads of the public and that they might have to try something safer first. Conversely, it was his mastery of engraving that recommended him to Stuart Crystal, the long-established firm of glass makers at Stourbridge, in the West Midlands. Stuart Crystal exhibited items of glassware by both Ravilious and Paul Nash at the 1934 Modern Art for the Table exhibition at Harrods, several of which were shown again the following year in the Exhibition of British Art and Industry at the Royal Academy. The modernist architect, Maxwell Fry, assisted by Ravilious, designed the 'Glassware' section for this exhibition, for which the latter created a series of decorative display panels with incised abstract pattern. In addition he exhibited eleven items including a decanter, a broad conical vase, cocktail shaker, several drinking glasses, plus a water jug and flower bowl. Since student days Ravilious had been interested in contemporary architecture and, in addition to Fry, had a number of

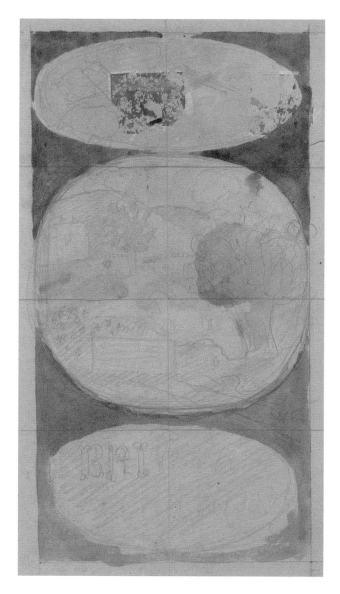

A preliminary design in pencil and watercolour, possibly commissioned by Stuarts Advertising Agency as a leaflet for British Airways (a branch of Imperial Airways) c1930s. The central panel illustrated a 'typical countryside view'.

architect friends including Serge Chermayeff, Oliver Hill and the architectural writer J.M Richards. Almost as an adjunct to the clean lines of modernist architecture, a number of young craftsmen during the 1930s were rediscovering the uncluttered simplicity of Regency design. This taste is reflected in the dining chairs and table, inlayed with elegant stringing and stars, that Ravilious designed for Dunbar Hay.

Lettering frequently played an integral rôle in his designs. In 1930 he designed and cut an upper-case alphabet for the Kynoch Press; the broad strokes of the dark letter forms, each decorated with a white curlicue. Such simple decoration, which he usually achieved through shading or the use of dotted lines, was to become a typical feature of his otherwise squarely formal capitals, while for lower-case lettering he tended to use a flowing script often with generous flourishes, as in his 1938 title page for The Writings of Gilbert White of Selborne. His letter-forms can be seen at their most idiosyncratic in the catalogue cover design he created the previous year for the Foreign Office for the Paris Exposition des Arts et Techniques dans la Vie Moderne, and for the British Pavilion at the 1939 New York World's Fair. For the Paris Exposition, working once again with Oliver Hill, he created a three-dimensional backdrop to the sports stand depicting a tennis match in progress watched by serried ranks of spectators. This was in many ways an extension of his earlier mural designs, but less pictorial, more stylised and more consciously an act of design; its rôle at the exhibition was a supporting one, it was there as background to a display of sports clothes.

After receiving confirmation of his attachment to the Royal Navy with the rank of captain in the Royal Marines on Christmas Eve 1939, the last three years of his life were largely taken up with his work as a war artist. He was first stationed at Chatham and then Sheerness in Kent, painting in and around the dockyards, before being transferred to Grimsby. The monotony of this land-based work was relieved in May 1940 when he joined the destroyer HMS Highlander, on a mission to the Arctic Circle. He was stimulated by this experience, the light and the novelty of the midnight sun excited him and with typical relish he compared the bombing to 'wonderful fireworks'[6] inspiring some of his finest watercolours. So, when in August 1942, following a spell back in Britain painting coastal defences, he was offered another chance to return to the Arctic region he seized it and joined, what was to be for him, a fateful expedition to Iceland. A few days after his arrival, on September 2nd, he had the chance to fly with an Air Sea Rescue plane from the RAF base Kaldadarnes in search of a missing seaplane, but his aircraft never returned. In the absence of any wreckage, he and the crew were at first declared missing, and it was not until March the following year that his death was officially confirmed.

Ravilious was just thirty-nine years old when he died. During the final months prior to the outbreak of war, he was bubbling with ideas, sketching designs for needlework, textiles, carpets, a penny stamp, even a child's handkerchief; if the war had not intervened there is no knowing what else he would have gone on to design. He was fastidious about everything that he drew, painted or designed. His designs, like his watercolours, are both timeless and classic.

Peyton Skipwith

1. Edward Bawden, *Eric Ravilious, The Minories*, Colchester, 1972
2. *Ibid*   3. *Ibid*
4. Harling, *Notes on the Wood Engravings of Eric Ravilious*, London,1946
5. Ravilious letters   6. *Ibid*

The RCA Students' Magazine. Title page engravings, above, December 1923, below, April 1924. Opposite, title page of *The Mandrake*, 1926, an RCA student magazine. Ravilious's *Bedroom* engraving was illustrated as a reduced line block.

¶THE MANDRAKE: A MAGAZINE
OF THE STUDENTS OF THE ROYAL COLLEGE
OF ART.   EDITED BY CECILIA A. DUNBAR
KILBURN : OF WHICH TWO HUNDRED COPIES
HAVE BEEN PRINTED, AND COLOURED BY
HAND, AND THE WHOLE PUT TOGETHER IN
MAY, MCMXXVI, THE MONTH AND YEAR
OF THE GREAT GENERAL STRIKE

Above, *Road at Florence*, 1924, below, *Cachine* 1924. Opposite, *Venus*, design detail for the Morley College murals, 1928.

The Royal College of Art diploma usually took three years to complete, but Ravilious's meagre grant meant he was required to complete the course in just two years. Nevertheless, he was awarded a distinction and won the Design School Travelling Scholarship. Winners were obliged to go to Italy – not Ravilious's first choice – to copy Italian paintings. Although he came back with only three engravings, the influence of his visits to chapels and galleries is obvious in his later work. On his return to England a further grant was found for him to complete his third year, just as Paul Nash arrived as a visiting tutor; his influence was to have a lasting effect on Ravilious.

indico river   purple and gold   salmon
                           franghin

Desert, a Legend by Martin Armstrong, published by Jonathan Cape, 1926. Ravilious's first illustrated book was published in ordinary and special editions in England and America. The American edition, printed on a smoother paper had better reproductions of the wood-engravings. Ravilious quickly learned to adapt his engravings to suit often inferior printing and the preference of private presses for printing on 'expensive' rough surface hand-made papers.

A Ballad upon a Wedding, by Sir John Suckling, published by Robert Gibbings'
Golden Cockerel Press, 1927. 375 copies were printed on Kelmscott hand-made
paper, Ravilious's first engravings for Gibbings. The book contains half a dozen small
vignettes illustrating the 17th century poem and this large and exuberant tailpiece.

Above, clockwise from top left, *February, April, July* and *June* from the *1929 Monotype Almanack* commissioned by Stanley Morrison, the firm's typographical adviser, and illustrated by Ravilious with signs of the Zodiac. Ravilious and Edward Bawden were working on the Morley College murals throughout 1928 as Ravilious was cutting the Almanack's blocks, and several of his themes – floating figures, and

the Sussex landscape with chalk figures – are repeated. *Muse*, 1928, top left, commissioned by Curwen as a bookmark for the Westminster Bank, was cut during Ravilious's work on the *Monotype Almanack* and bears striking similarities in design. Top right, *August*, bottom left, *October*, and bottom right, *December*, from the *1929 Monotype Almanack*.

Twelfth Night, 1932, published by Golden Cockerel Press, with 29 engravings printed in blue-grey and red-brown (disliked by Ravilious!) is one of the finest productions of Ravilious's work. The book also contains one of the earliest uses of the Golden Cockerel type especially designed by Eric Gill. First announced in 1931 the project had to be scaled down in size, quantity and price as the international financial situation worsened. Above, *Duke, one face, one voice, one habit and two persons* (Act V, Scene I). Below, Viola as a child. Opposite, announcement from the 1932 prospectus. The price of the book, announced in 1931, was 5 guineas.

TWELFTH
NIGHT
BY WILLIAM SHAKESPEARE

The engravings reproduced on this page are two of the smaller decorations which Eric Ravilious has cut for this edition. There are about 30 blocks which, printed in red or blue, are among this artist's best work. The size of the book is $13\frac{1}{4}$ x $9\frac{1}{2}$ins., the type is Golden Cockerel Face 14-point, the paper was specially made and watermarked for the press by Joseph Batchelor & Son, and the binding, $\frac{1}{2}$ red niger, special fabric sides, is by Sangorski & Sutcliffe. The edition is strictly limited, for both England and America, to 275 numbered copies, price 3 Guineas, & as with all other Golden Cockerel publications the type has been distributed after printing.

Above, *Twelfth Night* 1931, proof title page. Opposite, a sprite on his way to the 1932 Monotype Calendar, fireworks and a border of cockerels (which reappear as a repeat pattern binding cloth for the special edition of *Chanticleer: a Bibliography of the Golden Cockerel Press from April 1921 to August 1936*.) Feste sings 'When that I was and a little tiny boy' to end the play.

CLO. [Sings]
> When that I was and a little tiny boy,
>> With hey, ho, the wind and the rain,
> A foolish thing was but a toy,
>> For the rain it raineth every day.
>
> But when I came to man's estate,
>> With hey, ho, &c.
> 'Gainst knaves and thieves men shut their gate,
>> For the rain, &c.
>
> But when I came, alas! to wive,
>> With hey, ho, &c.
> By swaggering could I never thrive,
>> For the rain, &c.
>
> But when I came unto my beds,
>> With hey, ho, &c.
> With toss-pots still had drunken heads,
>> For the rain, &c.
>
> A great while ago the world begun,
>> With hey, ho, &c.
> But that's all one, our play is done,
>> And we'll strive to please you every day.

[Exit.

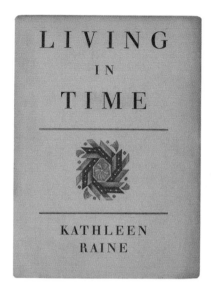
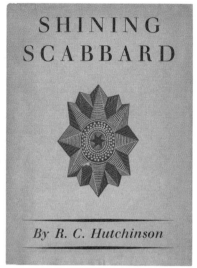

The Curwen 1930s stock blocks were held in the press composing room for use on printing jobs where decoration was required. Both jackets are set in Walbaum, a Curwen Press 'house' typeface. Left, *Catherine Wheel*, 1934, used on the dust jacket of Kathleen Raine's *Living in Time* published by Editions Poetry, London, 1946. Right, *Star*, 1936, used on the dust jacket of *Shining Scabbard* by R.C. Hutchinson, published by Cassell, 1936.

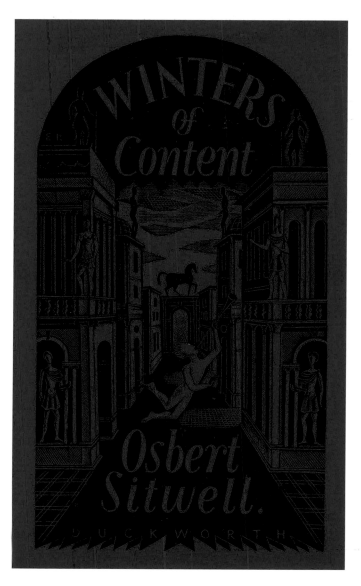

Winters of Content by Osbert Sitwell, 1932, dustwrapper for Duckworth's.

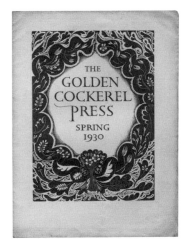

Golden Cockerel Prospectuses, 1930–33. The fairground cockerel rider, top right, is thought to be Tirzah Ravilious. The figure introducing the cockerel in the 1932 prospectus is Robert Gibbings, who loved his caricature.

Chanticleer, original drawing in pencil and watercolour
and wood-engraving for the 1931 spring prospectus.

MARCH 1933

SUNDAY		5	12	19	26	SUNDAY
MONDAY		6	13	20	27	MONDAY
TUESDAY		7	14	21	28	TUESDAY
WEDNESDAY	1	8	15	22	29	WEDNESDAY
THURSDAY	2	9	16	23	30	THURSDAY
FRIDAY	3	10	17	24	31	FRIDAY
SATURDAY	4	11	18	25		SATURDAY

THE MONOTYPE CORPORATION LIMITED, 43 FETTER LANE, LONDON :: SET IN TIMES NEW SERIES 327

APRIL 1933

SUNDAY	Mar26	2	9	16	23	30	SUNDAY
MONDAY	Mar27	3	10	17	24	May 1	MONDAY
TUESDAY	Mar28	4	11	18	25	May 2	TUESDAY
WEDNESDAY	Mar29	5	12	19	26	May 3	WEDNESDAY
THURSDAY	Mar30	6	13	20	27	May 4	THURSDAY
FRIDAY	Mar31	7	14	21	28	May 5	FRIDAY
SATURDAY	1	8	15	22	29	May 6	SATURDAY

THE MONOTYPE CORPORATION LTD., 43 FETTER LANE, LONDON :: SET IN BELL 341

MAY, 1933

SUNDAY		7	14	21	28	SUNDAY
MONDAY	1	8	15	22	29	MONDAY
TUESDAY	2	9	16	23	30	TUESDAY
WEDNESDAY	3	10	17	24	31	WEDNESDAY
THURSDAY	4	11	18	25		THURSDAY
FRIDAY	5	12	19	26		FRIDAY
SATURDAY	6	13	20	27		SATURDAY

THE MONOTYPE CORPORATION LTD., 43 FETTER LANE, LONDON :: PERPETUA TITLING 258

THE ILLUSTRATIONS ARE FROM ORIGINAL WOOD-ENGRAVINGS BY ERIC RAVILIOUS

JUNE, 1933

SUNDAY		4	11	18	25	SUNDAY
MONDAY	MAY 29	5	12	19	26	MONDAY
TUESDAY	MAY 30	6	13	20	27	TUESDAY
WEDNESDAY	MAY 31	7	14	21	28	WEDNESDAY
THURSDAY	1	8	15	22	29	THURSDAY
FRIDAY	2	9	16	23	30	FRIDAY
SATURDAY	3	10	17	24	JULY 1	SATURDAY

THE MONOTYPE CORPORATION LTD, 43 FETTER LANE, E.C.4 :: GOUDY MOD. 249

ILLUSTRATIONS ARE FROM ORIGINAL WOOD-ENGRAVINGS BY ERIC RAVILIOUS

Monotype Calendar, 1933.

JULY, 1933

SUNDAY	June 25	2	9	16	23	30		SUNDAY
MONDAY	June 26	3	10	17	24	31		MONDAY
TUESDAY	June 27	4	11	18	25	Aug. 1		TUESDAY
WEDNESDAY	June 28	5	12	19	26	Aug. 2		WEDNESDAY
THURSDAY	June 29	6	13	20	27	Aug. 3		THURSDAY
FRIDAY	June 30	7	14	21	28	Aug. 4		FRIDAY
SATURDAY		1	8	15	22	29	Aug. 5	SATURDAY

THE MONOTYPE CORPORATION LTD., 43 FETTER LANE, LONDON :: SET IN BODONI 135

THE ILLUSTRATIONS ARE FROM ORIGINAL WOOD-ENGRAVINGS BY ERIC RAVILIOUS

Monotype Calendar, 1933.

SUNDAY	JULY 30	6	13	20	27		SUNDAY
MONDAY	JULY 31	7	14	21	28		MONDAY
TUESDAY	1	8	15	22	29		TUESDAY
WEDNESDAY	2	9	16	23	30		WEDNESDAY
THURSDAY	3	10	17	24	31		THURSDAY
FRIDAY	4	11	18	25	SEPT. 1		FRIDAY
SATURDAY	5	12	19	26	SEPT. 2		SATURDAY

THE MONOTYPE CORPORATION LTD., 43 FETTER LANE, E.C.4 :: BASKERVILLE 169

ILLUSTRATIONS ARE FROM ORIGINAL WOOD-ENGRAVINGS BY ERIC RAVILIOUS

Monotype Calendar, 1933.

SEPTEMBER, 1933

SUNDAY	Aug 27	3	10	17	24	SUNDAY
MONDAY	Aug 28	4	11	18	25	MONDAY
TUESDAY	Aug 29	5	12	19	26	TUESDAY
WEDNESDAY	Aug 30	6	13	20	27	WEDNESDAY
THURSDAY	Aug 31	7	14	21	28	THURSDAY
FRIDAY	1	8	15	22	29	FRIDAY
SATURDAY	2	9	16	23	30	SATURDAY

THE MONOTYPE CORPORATION LTD, 43 FETTER LANE, E.C.4 :: BEMBO 270

ILLUSTRATIONS FROM ORIGINAL WOOD-ENGRAVINGS BY ERIC RAVILIOUS

OCTOBER 1933

SUNDAY	1	8	15	22	29	SUNDAY
MONDAY	2	9	16	23	30	MONDAY
TUESDAY	3	10	17	24	31	TUESDAY
WEDNESDAY	4	11	18	25	NOV 1	WEDNESDAY
THURSDAY	5	12	19	26	NOV 2	THURSDAY
FRIDAY	6	13	20	27	NOV 3	FRIDAY
SATURDAY	7	14	21	28	NOV 4	SATURDAY

THE MONOTYPE CORPORATION LTD, 43 FETTER LANE, LONDON :: GILL EXTRA-LIGHT 362

THE ILLUSTRATIONS ARE FROM ORIGINAL WOOD-ENGRAVINGS BY ERIC RAVILIOUS

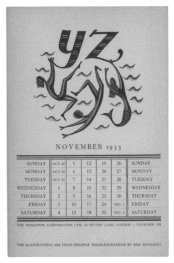

NOVEMBER 1933

SUNDAY	OCT. 29	5	12	19	26	SUNDAY
MONDAY	OCT. 30	6	13	20	27	MONDAY
TUESDAY	OCT. 31	7	14	21	28	TUESDAY
WEDNESDAY	1	8	15	22	29	WEDNESDAY
THURSDAY	2	9	16	23	30	THURSDAY
FRIDAY	3	10	17	24	DEC. 1	FRIDAY
SATURDAY	4	11	18	25	DEC. 2	SATURDAY

THE MONOTYPE CORPORATION LTD, 43 FETTER LANE, LONDON :: FOURNIER 185

THE ILLUSTRATIONS ARE FROM ORIGINAL WOOD-ENGRAVINGS BY ERIC RAVILIOUS

DECEMBER 1933

SUNDAY	Nov. 26	3	10	17	24	31	SUNDAY
MONDAY	Nov. 27	4	11	18	25	Jan. 1	MONDAY
TUESDAY	Nov. 28	5	12	19	26	Jan. 2	TUESDAY
WEDNESDAY	Nov. 29	6	13	20	27	Jan. 3	WEDNESDAY
THURSDAY	Nov. 30	7	14	21	28	Jan. 4	THURSDAY
FRIDAY	1	8	15	22	29	Jan. 5	FRIDAY
SATURDAY	2	9	16	23	30	Jan. 6	SATURDAY

THE MONOTYPE CORPN LTD, 43 FETTER LANE, E.C.4 :: POLIPHILUS 170

ILLUSTRATIONS ARE FROM ORIGINAL WOOD-ENGRAVINGS BY ERIC RAVILIOUS

Monotype Calendar, 1933.

Enter Barabas in his counting-house, with heapes of gold before him	Barabas (The Jew of Malta): *Oh my girle, my gold, my fortune, my felicity;*

The Famous Tragedy of the Rich Jew of Malta, 1933. Although not the most beautiful piece of book design and production, Ravilious's four large engravings for the book are exquisitely designed and cut and he wrote that he was pleased with them. *The Jew of Malta*, written by Christopher Marlowe, 1633, printed at the Chiswick Press and published by the Golden House

Ithamore (a Turkish slave): *Content,*
but we will leaue this paltry land,
And saile from hence to Greece, to
louely Greece.

A charge. the
cable cut, a
Caldron discouered

Press in 1933, was planned as a deluxe production with a specially marbled
binding cloth, leather spine and corners. Very few seem to have sold and the
remainders were bound in green buckram and sold at discounted prices.
Whether this was bad marketing, lack of popularity of Marlowe or the financial
depression isn't recorded. The speakers' lines and stage directions are from
Marlowe's text spellings.

Architecture Illustrated magazine devoted its September 1933 issue to The Midland Hotel, Morecambe. The hotel was designed by Oliver Hill, Eric Gill carved reliefs, Marion Dorn designed mosaics and Ravilious, assisted by his wife Tirzah, painted murals. The magazine described 'An unique feature of the scheme, though independent of the hotel, is the circular café adjacent to and overlooking the site of the proposed new swimming pool. This has accommodation for seating, within and on the terrace, some two hundred people at a sitting and also has a dancing floor. The walls are entirely covered in frescoes, painted by Eric Ravilious, representing morning, noon and night, in an idyllic seascape setting.' The tabular metal furniture cellulosed putty colour, table tops shell pink vitrolite, and floors walnut.

A Christmas
Shopping List
from
The Little Gallery
3 Ellis Street
Sloane Street
S.W.1

Telephone: Sloane 6663

CHRISTMAS

1933

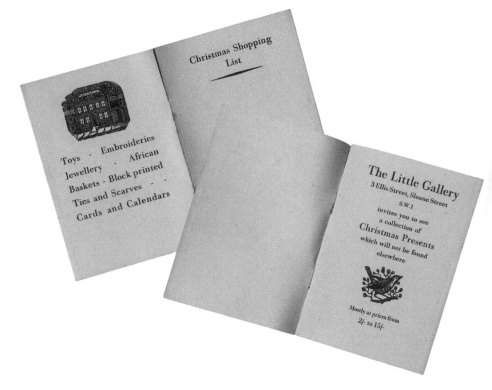

Christmas Shopping
List

Toys - Embroideries
Jewellery - African
Baskets - Block printed
Ties and Scarves -
Cards and Calendars

The Little Gallery
3 Ellis Street, Sloane Street
S.W.1
invites you to see
a collection of
Christmas Presents
which will not be found
elsewhere

Mostly at prices from
2/- to 15/-

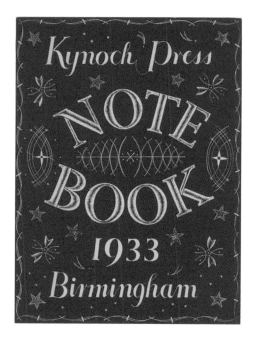

Muriel Rose, a friend of Ravilious and owner of The Little Gallery, produced a small *Christmas Shopping List*, opposite, printed from the 1933 *Kynoch Press Note Book* wood blocks, title page above. The Kynoch Press was owned by ICI and printed the company's publicity and packaging. The annual *Note Book* was published to promote its printing services to outside clients. Ravilious had also designed and cut a rather quirky alphabet of initials for the Press in 1930, below. Although rarely used, the letters work well spelling Ravilious's name on the dust jacket of the *Engravings by Eric Ravilious*, 1946, by Robert Harling.

Fifty-Four Conceits, verses by Martin Armstrong, published by Martin Secker, 1933. The engravings are repeated throughout the book.

The aeroplane above was reused on Wedgwood *Travel* ceramics and in *Poems by Thomas Hennell*, published by Oxford University Press, 1936.

Booklets and stationery printed by the Curwen and Kynoch Presses, 1930s.

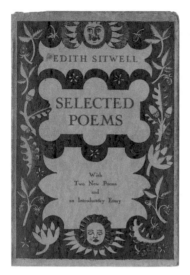

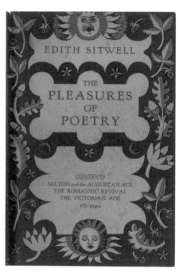

Fireworks and flowers, book jackets all for Duckworth's, publishers, 1930s.

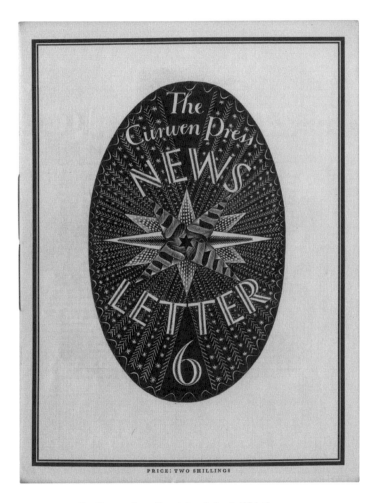

PRICE: TWO SHILLINGS

The Curwen Press Newsletter 6, April 1934, the
magazine ran to 15 issues between 1932 and 1939.

British Art, BBC talks pamphlet, 1934. Printed by
Kynoch who presumably commissioned Ravilious.

Cecilia Dunbar Kilburn (later Lady Forbes-Sempill), had been a sculpture student at the RCA with Bawden, Bliss and Ravilious. She and Athole Hay, the RCA registrar, opened Dunbar Hay in 1936 with the objective of commissioning and selling work by contemporary designers. Ravilious was put on a retainer and designed printed material, textiles, furniture and ceramics for Wedgwood, commissioned through Dunbar's friendship with the

Wedgwood family. Opposite, 'Doll's House' trade card, 1938, wood-engraving transferred to lithography. Ravilious played with scale to show a range of the shop's wares: furniture, cutlery, glassware, giant teapot and rolls of fabric. Above, a large scale watercolour design for a carpet, with ribboned border and sponged fringe, late 1930s. The central motif of figs is surrounded by decorations of strawberries, cherries, hops (twice) and a pencilled *cassis*.

Top, *The Beauty of Southern England*, middle, *The Birthplace of English History*, bottom, *Social and Sporting Season*. The *Crown and Sceptre* wrapping paper, opposite, was commissioned by Curwen for Heals as a 1935 Royal Jubilee celebration. The repeat pattern was reused, probably due to a tight deadline, by the Southern Railway with engraved headpieces for *Thrice Welcome* a booklet, left, 'primarily for the assistance of Overseas Visitors visiting this country for the Jubilee'.

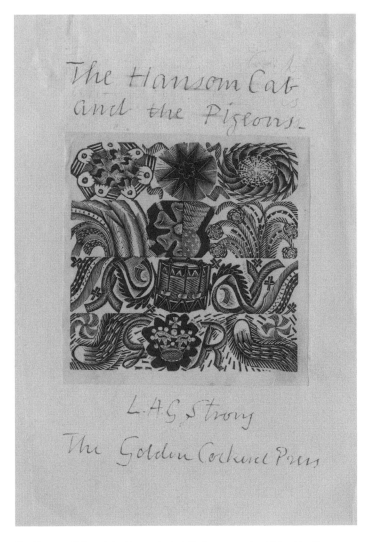

The Hansom Cab and the Pigeons by L.A.G. Strong, and published by the Golden Cockerel Press for the Jubilee of King George V, 1935. Strong's story of a pigeon-inhabited hansom cab suited Ravilious's relish in junk-yards, '... to have a job of this sort at all is heartening' he wrote to the publisher. Above, an unused cover design, and chapter heading and frontispiece, opposite.

Above, *Pony and Trap* or *Miss Creed of Little Bardfield*, 1935, Redfern Publishing.
Below, *Double Crown Club* menu, 1935, illustrating the food eaten at the dinner.

Poems by Thomas Hennell, published by Oxford University Press, 1936. In an edition of only 50 illustrated copies. Above, *Island,* below, *Flower Thanksgiving,* based on a tomb effigy in Little Easton Church, Essex.

Proposed designs for Wedgwood, *Leaves and Grasses*, 1936, above and *Ribbon*, 1937, below.

Above, *Troy*, originally designed in 1936 and produced in bone china, 1952.
Below, *Persephone*, introduced in 1936, as earthenware in several colourways,
was produced as *Golden Persephone*, on bone china for the 1953 Coronation.

The *Garden Implements* jug, above, was introduced by Wedgwood in 1939 as a lemonade set with 6 beakers. The engravings were reused on a printed cotton fabric, opposite, produced by Edinburgh Weavers after World War II. It came in a variety of colourways and finishes, shown here printed blue on glazed cotton. The vignettes appear on the reverse of the jug.

London Transport booklets, 1936. Designed to encourage city dwellers to take tubes and buses to explore the countryside around London. The booklets were designed by Robert Harling, London Transport's typographical adviser and friend of Ravilious (Harling had asked him to cut the *Wisden Cricketers' Almanack* engraving).

Above, engravings for use in London Transport's Greenline buses advertising, 1935. Right, *Afternoon Tea*, introduced by Wedgwood in 1938.

For the United Kingdom pavilion at the 1937 Paris Exhibition, again working with Oliver Hill, Ravilious was commissioned to create a three-dimensional set in paint and cardboard, as a backdrop to display sportswear. The original design, above, was reduced to a surreal tennis match, below left. The Foreign Office also commissioned Ravilious to design and engrave the illuminated 'GR pavilion' as catalogue covers, left, in both English and French versions. Ravilious wrote 'could I tell them [the committee] that the GR is for Ginger Rogers?'

Chapter headings for the *Country Life Cookery Book*, 1937.

Ravilious cut only eleven engravings and repeated *January*.

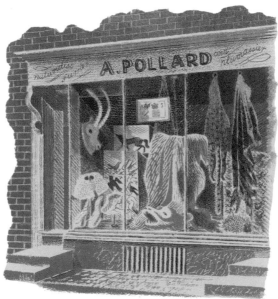

Three trial lithographs for what was to become *High Street*, published by *Country Life* in 1938, were printed in *Signature* magazine in 1937. The illustrations, each reproduced from four printing plates, appeared softer in the magazine than those in the book. John Piper, who had published Ravilious's *Newhaven Harbour* print at Contemporary Lithographs, wrote the short accompanying text. J.M. Richards, editor of the *Architectural Review*, later wrote a lighthearted description for each of the illustrations in the 1938 book.

The Reverend Gilbert White's two-volume *Selborne* was Ravilious's last major engraved work and his only book for the Nonesuch Press, published in 1938.

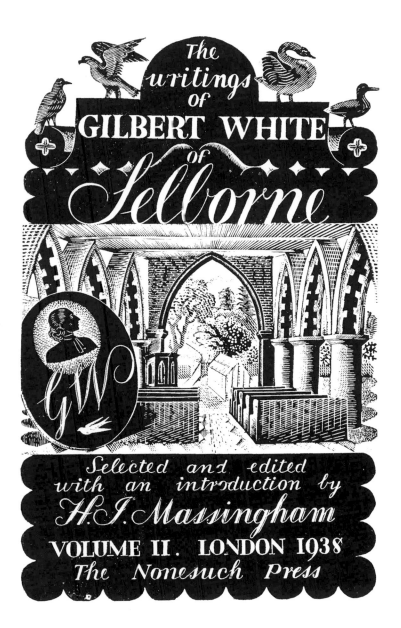

Although the threat of war was not far off, *Beautiful Britain*, the 1939 *Country Life Calendar*, would have been in production in early 1938. The calendar, with a three colour lithograph by Ravilious and reproductions of black and white photographs for each week of the year, was printed by Morrison and Gibb. The photography reflects idyllic, pre-war, English country life: Kentish oast houses, primroses in spring and views of the Lake District. Ironically, the first January photograph is of a Georgian mansion entitled 'An Englishman's Home'. The 1940 calendar, with a cover by John Nash, included similar photographs to that of 1939, possibly in defiance of imminent invasion.

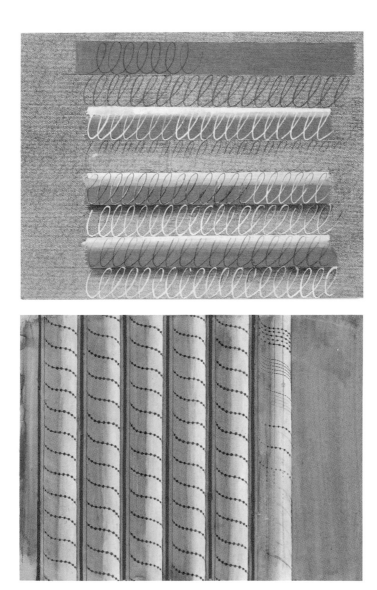

Working designs, watercolour, for pattern papers or
possibly textile patterns for the Cotton Board, c1941.

As well as tennis, Ravilious's vocabulary of favourite motifs appear throughout his design work: fireworks, illuminations and pavilions. Above, design for an unpublished work that includes the flags of the allies (with an uncharacteristic scribbled title). Clients' tight deadlines are an obvious reason for using existing references, but his themes adapt and develop with use on paper, textiles and ceramics. Opposite, national symbols and architectural illuminations combine to illustrate the lithographed jacket for *London Fabric*, by James Pope-Hennessy, published by Batsford in 1939. Although not credited, the typesetting in Walbaum on the flaps would suggest the jacket was lithographed at Curwen.

James Pope-Hennessy

LONDON
FABRIC

Postage stamp designs for Royal Mail. Above, although dated 1928, design for the 1929 *Postal Union Congress £1* stamp. Ravilious's floating figures supporting the lower ribbon are closely related to his Morley College mural. The central frame would have contained a portrait of King George V. This rather lightweight design was rejected in favour of the monumentally large design by Harold Nelson.

Commissioned before the outbreak of war, above, design for the commemorative stamp to celebrate the centenary of the Penny Black. The approved design was a simple double portrait of Queen Victoria and King George VI. The design's arches, an idea used for the Barlaston mug, contains on the left an illustrated pavilion, topped by a crown and on the right, the George VI profile. Opposite, Ravilious's collaged proof cover design for the New York World Fair catalogue, 1939. The first design proposal, described in a letter from Ravilious to A.J.A. Symons as 'my podgy Britannia', was rejected with a request for a coat of arms. The catalogue was entirely revised when war was declared and Ravilious cut a new date for the 1940 edition.

HONI SOIT QUI MAL Y PENSE

DIEU ET MON DROIT

1939

THE BRITISH PAVILION

The 1937 Edward VIII Coronation mug, top, was Ravilious's first commission from Wedgwood. It was withdrawn at news of the abdication (Mrs Simpson was rumoured to have already bought one at Dunbar Hay). The artwork was revised for the coronation of King George VI, and then again for the 1953 coronation of Queen Elizabeth II. Middle, *Alphabet* nursery set, introduced in 1937, the colour bands came in various colours. Barlaston mug, bottom, was introduced in 1940 to celebrate the re-location of the factory. The illustrations are from *The Architectural Review*, December 1943.

The rough design and finished engraving for *English Wits*, published in 1940 by Hutchinson, is, as its title suggests, a book of wit and biography, by other wits and biographers: Wyndham Lewis on Whistler (American!), Harold Hobson on George Bernard Shaw etc. The editor Leonard Russell wrote to Ravilious asking for designs within three weeks; Ravilious did them in two.

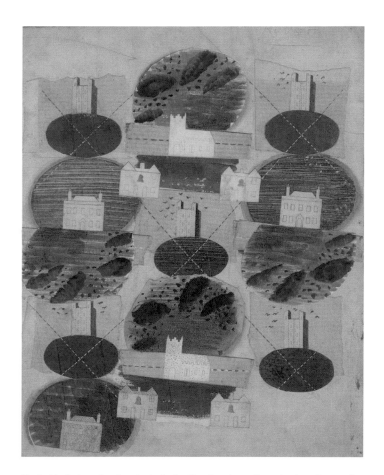

Castle Hedingham Landmarks, including the church, castle and pub, collage and watercolour for the Cotton Board, 1941. The Ravilious family moved from Great Bardfield to Castle Hedingham in 1934. Another design not put into production, the pattern repeat is of a large scale, Ravilious jokingly complained in a letter that women only wanted patterns the size of threepenny bits.

Opposite, one of the small number of designs for textiles commissioned by
the wartime Cotton Board organisation (the only Ravilious design that got
as far as limited production was a children's handkerchief). Above, a small
watercolour and pencil design for a fabric, 1941. The 'cube' and ears of wheat
relate to the design opposite. The origin of the cube was possibly a design
for the *Cactus House* (what looks like a turret is just
visible in pale pencil) that Ravilious produced for
Paul Nash's 1932 *Room and Book* exhibition held at
the Zwemmer Gallery, London. On the same sheet
are very early drawings for a nautical symbol textile.
Right, Britannia holding a star, pencil.

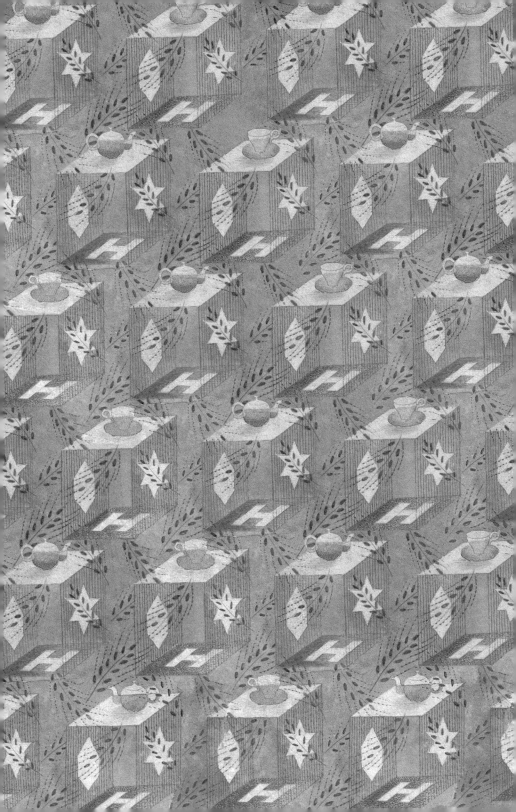

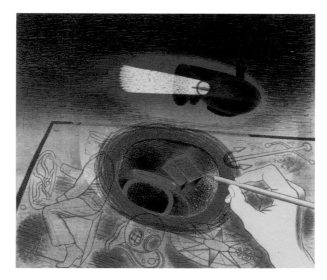

Originally planned as a children's painting book, described in a letter 'to persuade boys to go into the navy', Ravilious's ten submarine lithographs, 1941–42, became a personal and last lithographic print project. The Curwen Press, printers of most of his lithographic jobs including *High Street*, having been bombed, the series was printed by Cowell's of Ipswich.

Engravings commissioned for the *Weekly Intelligence Report*, a wartime
publication listing naval activities, 1942. Robert Harling, who was now working
at the Admiralty was instrumental in commissioning these last engravings
from Ravilious. *WIR* was not declassified until 2002, but
two 'uncleared' blocks of Ravilious's engravings were
used on the front cover of the *Architectural Review*
in December 1943, right, illustrated together with
engravings from the 1933 Kynoch Press Note
Book. The magazine carried an obituary and
an extensive article on Ravilious's work as a
designer by the architect Robert Goodden.

Top, *Britain's Increased Production* and, above, *The Empire Air Training Scheme*, collage and gouache diagrams. Designs for wartime publications, c1941.

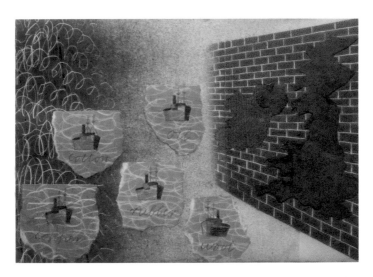

Top, *They Do Not Reach Germany* and, above, *Industrial Strength Since the Last War*, collage and gouache diagrams. Designs for wartime publications, c1941.

Invitations and catalogues to one-man exhibitions held during Ravilious's lifetime and for his Brighton and Eastbourne Memorial Exhibition, 1948.

Afterword

t is ironic that until his centenary exhibition at the Imperial War Museum in 2003 Eric Ravilious, one of Britain's finest twentieth-century artists, was best known through two of his design classics, the Coronation and Alphabet mugs for Wedgwood. During his life he had just three exhibitions, two at the Zwemmer Gallery – 1933 & 1936 – and a final one with Arthur Tooth & Son in 1939, showing ninety-eight watercolours in total, priced at no more than twenty-five guineas (£26.25p). Following his death the public had to wait six years to see the Memorial Exhibitions, after which there was little further interest in his work until the large-scale retrospective mounted by the Minories in Colchester in 1972, which toured to Morley College, London, the Ashmolean Museum, Oxford and the Towner Gallery, Eastbourne. Since then his star has been firmly in the ascendant with major exhibitions of his work at the Fry Art Gallery (1992, 2003 and 2011), The Fine Art Society (2002), Imperial War Museum (2003), Towner, Eastbourne (2010) and Dulwich (2015). Publications have followed the same trajectory, starting with the modest tribute by Helen Binyon and reaching a peak with the three monumental volumes of letters edited by his daughter, Anne Ullmann, and others, plus Tirzah Garwood's Long Live Great Bardfield & Love to You all, published by the Fleece Press, which have been augmented by Jeremy Greenwood's equally monumental catalogue raisonné and the Ravilious in Pictures series from the Mainstone Press.

Acknowledgements

Design for Morley College murals, p.8 and p.27, private collection. Designs for textile patterns, p.79 and wartime publications, p.92, The Wolfsonian-FIU Museum. Postage stamp designs p.82, reproduced with kind permission of Royal Mail Group Ltd and the British Postal Museum and Archive.

Self-portrait, overleaf, 1941–42. Ravilious's own hand, drawn for the Introductory Lithograph from his series of submarine prints. Decorated inital, above, from Transitions, poems by Mabel Huddleston, 1936, printed by Guido Morris and Beatrice Warde.

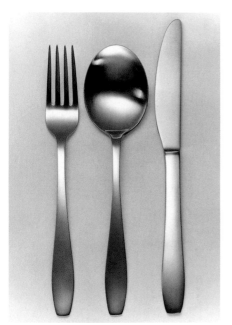 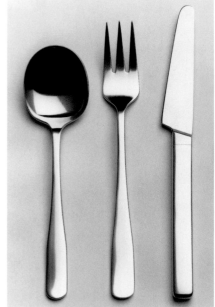

Campden (or Spring) (left), stainless steel, 1956, designed by David Mellor and Robert Welch. One of the first results of his new role as design consultant at Walker & Hall, on this design Mellor collaborated with his RCA contemporary Robert Welch whose career in cutlery has in some ways paralleled Mellor's own.

Symbol (right), won the designer his third Design Centre Award, manufactured by Walker & Hall at their new Bolsover factory, 1961. *Symbol* was Mellor's first high quality stainless steel design, 'strong and consistent right through, resists wear as neither silver nor silver plating will. The visual and tactile qualities are not just on the surface.'

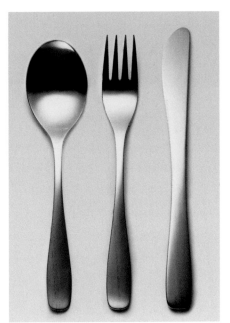 

One of Mellor's most important designs, *Thrift* (left) was commissioned in 1965 for government canteens from prisons to hospitals. The designer had produced a stainless steel cutlery set that was thoroughly modern, socially radical and reduced manufacturing costs but it was *Thrift*'s universal reach that pleased him most, 'The chances are that the spoon in the average civil servant's saucer will be mine and I like to think the design has honest quality'.

Odeon, (right), a rectilinear and purist design of 1986, makes reference to the Bauhaus functionalism of the 1920s, but with 1980s glitter. Made from heavyweight stainless steel with a highly polished finish.

The construction of the Round Building. Set in the Peak District National Park, the factory, home, shop, café and museum expresses Mellor's philosophy of living and working being seamlessly intertwined, as well as the belief that visual dialogues between the traditional and the modern, the domestic and the industrial could be beautiful.

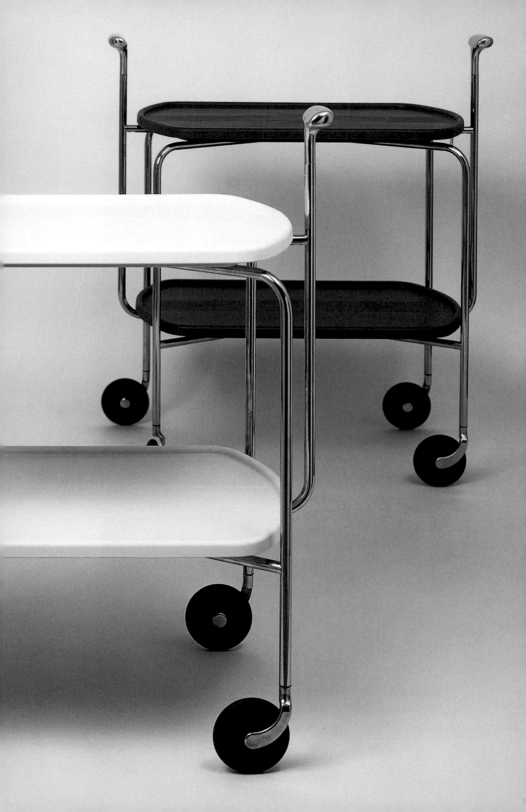

Prototype chair for Magis, stainless steel and blow moulded plastic, 2000.
A strikingly contemporary design by David Mellor at the age of 70.

Transit trolley (opposite) by David and Corin Mellor for Magis, Italy, 1998.

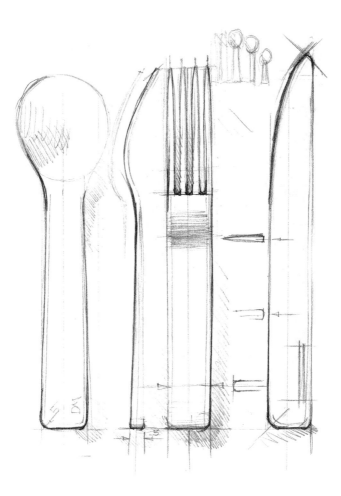

Minimal, stainless steel, 2002. One of Mellor's most aesthetically radical designs, he explained, 'In almost fifty years of cutlery design... I have been hoping one day to arrive at the absolute minimal set made to the finest possible standards... Though basic in concept I wanted to get away from the idea of rigorous functional austerity with this design.'

Embassy glassware (top), by Corin Mellor, 2008 and *Linear* glassware (above), by Corin Mellor, 2007. Black-handled kitchen knives (opposite), by Corin Mellor, 2007. Corin Mellor continues and expands upon the design approaches of his father. In the instance of *Embassy* glassware his products compliment the original designs; whether additions or 'Corin Mellor originals' his work exudes a contemporary freshness that keeps the family business moving forward.

Chronology

1930	Born in Sheffield, 5 October 1930. Parents Colin and Ivy (neé Rogerson) Mellor.
1935	Lydgate Lane and then Crookes Endowed School.
1942	Junior Art Department of Sheffield College of Art.
1945	Sheffield College of Art.
1948	Start of studies at Royal College of Art delayed by 18 months' National Service.
1950	Royal College of Art, London.
1952	Travelling scholarship to Scandinavia and Germany.
1953	Studied at British School at Rome.
1954	Left Royal College of Art with Silver Medal.
	Set up first workshop in Eyre Street, Sheffield.
	Appointed design consultant to the Sheffield cutlery manufacturer Walker & Hall.
1957	Pride cutlery for Walker & Hall included in first Design Centre Awards.
1959	Design Centre Award for Grahamston Ironfounders' Queen room heater.
1960	Commissioned modern purpose-built studio-workshop in Sheffield from Patric Guest of Gollins Melvin Ward.
1962	Elected Royal Designer for Industry.
	Design Centre Award for Symbol cutlery for Walker & Hall.
1964	Fellow of Society of Industrial Artists and Designers.
1965-69	Consultant to Ministry of Transport on design of national traffic signals system.
1965	Design Centre Award for Embassy sterling silver tableware.
1966	Design Centre Award for Thrift stainless steel cutlery.
	Controversial new square pillar box commissioned by the Post Office.
	Married Fiona MacCarthy, biographer and critic.
	Son Corin born.
	Hon. Fellow of Royal College of Art.
1969	Opened first London shop, David Mellor, Ironmonger, Sloane Square, followed by shops in Manchester, Covent Garden and Butler's Wharf.
1970	Daughter Clare born.

1972	Exhibition at National Museum of Wales.	1986	Hon. D.Litt,. University of Sheffield.
1973	Set up workshops for specialist cutlery production at Broom Hall, Sheffield.	1988	Chartered Society of Designers Medal.
1975	Design Council Award for Abacus 700 outdoor seating.	1990	Completion of the Round Building cutlery factory.
1977	Design Council Award for Chinese Ivory cutlery.	1992	David Mellor Country Shop opened at Hathersage
1979	Designer of exhibition 'A Century of British Design 1880-1980' at Mappin Gallery, Sheffield.	1994	David Mellor Design in finals of European Commission Design Prize.
	Hon. Fellow of Sheffield City Polytechnic (now Sheffield Hallam University).	1997	Hon. D. Design, De Montfort University.
1981	Appointed OBE.	1998	Major retrospective exhibition at the Design Museum, London, and the Mappin Art Gallery, Sheffield and Dean Clough Galleries, Halifax.
	Liveryman of Worshipful Company of Goldsmiths.		
	Freeman of Cutlers' Company.	1999	Hon. Dr., Royal College of Art.
	Royal Society of Arts Presidential Award for Design Management.	2001	Appointed CBE.
		2006	Opening of David Mellor Design Museum at Hathersage.
1981-83	Chairman of Design Council Committee of Inquiry into Standards of Design in Consumer Goods in Britain.		Hon. Dr. of Technology, Loughborough University.
			V&A / Homes & Garden Lifetime Achievement Award 'for a significant and enduring contribution to domestic product design in Britain'.
1982-84	Chairman of Crafts Council.		
1983-88	Trustee of Victoria & Albert Museum.	2009	David Mellor died 7 May.